kid chef junior every day

kid chef junior EVERY DAY

MY First EASY KIDS' COOKBOOK

Yaffi Lvova, RDN

PHOTOGRAPHY BY ELYSA WEITALA

ROCKRIDGE PRESS

For you, Little Chef.

Continue to approach the world with curiosity, adventure, and whisk in hand.

And for my own little chefs:

Shimmy, Ben, and Daniel and Mae, Natan, and Liran

First Rockridge Press hardcover edition 2022

Originally published in trade paperback by Rockridge Press 2021

For general information on our other products and services, please contact our Customer Care Department within the United States at (866) 744-2665, or outside the United States at (510) 253-0500.

Hardcover ISBN: 979-8-88650-466-8
Paperback ISBN: 978-1-63807-328-4
eBook ISBN: 978-1-63807-221-8

Manufactured in the United States of America

Interior and Cover Designer: Brieanna Felschow
Art Producer: Sara Feinstein
Editor: Laura Apperson
Production Editor: Emily Sheehan
Production Manager: Holly Haydash

Photography © 2021 Elysa Weitala.
Food styling by Victoria Woollard.

10 9 8 7 6 5 4 3 2 1 0

CONTENTS

··

Chapter 1:
KIDS IN THE KITCHEN
EVERY DAY

Chapter 2:
BREAKFAST

Chapter 5:

DESSERTS & DRINKS 89

A NOTE TO GROWN-UPS

Hi there! I'm Yaffi —mother, dietitian, and creator of Toddler Test Kitchen™. I never thought I would be teaching kids how to cook. I still remember a time in my life when cooking was a source of stress. Dinner took me two hours to prepare— and it was nothing to look at.

In the kitchen, surrounded by the warm, comforting aromas, you can teach your children who they are: Recreate special family recipes and recount stories from your grandmother's table. Make new memories and strengthen links to the past at the same time. Stir up some culture by revisiting recipe books specific to your background and history.

By handing over the whisk, you can show your child you have confidence in them. Using this book is the perfect place to begin. These recipes are simple and delicious. They represent all five flavors detected by the human tongue:

1. Sweet
2. Salty
3. Bitter
4. Sour
5. Umami (a Japanese word commonly translated as "savory")

When eaten together around the dinner table, food serves to bolster the very essence of *family*: sharing the joy and comfort of a meal, spending time with loved ones, and feeling safe and supported. Who wouldn't want a bite of that?

Cooking can be fun and educational. It can build self-esteem and increase the chance of a child trying something unfamiliar. As I say at Toddler Test Kitchen™, "It's all about the smile, not the bite."

Cooking is an activity, and, as such, there are some ducks you want to have in a row before beginning. To maximize fun and minimize stress, keep the following guidelines in mind:

1. **Mind the schedule!** Cooking takes time. If you're in a rush, it won't be any fun. Prep and cook times are calculated as if an adult were cooking. Kids often take longer, so be sure to account for that.

2. **Cooking is seriously sensory.** Kids should feel free to taste as they go. A child who is hesitant to eat something new at the table may have no problem at all tasting that same ingredient when cooking. This is mainly because there is absolutely no pressure to eat—this lack of pressure can leave a selective child feeling more adventurous. It's also a good reason to have extra ingredients on hand.

3. **Take a step back.** Just like learning to walk or read, learning how to cook is a process. Kids have to make mistakes in order to grow, and they will make mistakes in the kitchen. Unless there is an immediate safety concern, allow them to make these missteps. It's how they will learn and build confidence. Don't be a backseat chef!

4. **Clean as you go.** Whistle while you work and clean the dishes as you go. Get the kids on board so you're not left with a tornado of a kitchen on the other side. As a bonus, cleaning up from cooking actually provides a child with additional exposure to unfamiliar ingredients, which may result in a greater willingness to try that food when it's ready!

5. **It's all in the expectations!** So much of parenting comes down to expectations, and cooking is no different. Consider your child's attention span. Discuss the recipe prior to starting: How long is this going to take? How long will it have to bake . . . and then cool before we can have a taste? If a recipe isn't going well, it's okay. Let your little one run around in the backyard while you finish it up. Try together again on another day. Just like with any other activity, sometimes you have to pivot!

6. **Embrace the perfection of imperfection.** It won't be perfect. But it's perfect to your mini chef. The smile that comes with "I made it myself" is priceless. Besides, a delicious mess is still delicious.

7. **Start slowly.** The goal is a tasty meal and a great smile. If your child is new to the kitchen, start off with the simpler recipes and allow them to build their skills and confidence as you work through this book.

8. **Grow a chef!** Rome wasn't built in a day, right? The more you cook together, the better you'll get at stepping back and the better your child will get at cooking. Nothing tastes better than a meal cooked by your smiling little chef.

Kid Chef Junior Every Day is all about providing your family with food that kids like to eat often and that is relatively easy to make. It's also a resource for recipes that grow with your child's skills and confidence in the kitchen. Start out with the Easy recipes and work toward the Medium or Hard recipes as your child conquers each skill.

For younger kids, start by reading them "A Note to Kids," which comes right after this section. Tour your kitchen together, showing your child where the necessary equipment lives. Read through chapter 1, "Kids in the Kitchen Every Day" (page 1) together and discuss kitchen rules, safety, and equipment. Whenever you see a (STOP) symbol, it means your help may be needed to complete a step, like taking a hot pan out of the oven or using a sharp knife.

If your child reads, you can hand over this book and go relax—within shouting distance, anyway. This book is meant to support independence, and the reading child is ready for that step.

Keep in mind that kids are impulsive. If you show them this book, chances are they will want to *do it right now*. So, choose your timing carefully.

One final note: Have fun! Remember, it's all about the smiles.

"Cooking with kids is not just about ingredients, recipes, and cooking. It's about harnessing imagination, empowerment, and creativity."

— Guy Fieri

A NOTE TO KIDS

Did you know that you can cook? You really can—and you're about to prove it to yourself. Whether cooking is a new activity, or you've been at it for a long time already, this book is for you.

Each recipe is rated Easy, Medium, or Hard. This will help you decide how much you can do on your own. Sometimes you'll see a symbol. This means you should STOP and ask a grown-up for help. The step may be a bit difficult, and I want you to be super safe.

When my father was in the kitchen, he'd cook up something delicious, but he never wrote down what he did. He had to rely on his memory the next time he wanted to make it, and sometimes he just couldn't remember what he'd done before. Don't make the same mistake. Write notes next to each recipe:

- **Who helped you cook?**
- **Did you love the recipe?**
- **Did you change the recipe while cooking?**

Cooking is not all serious, though. The best seasoning for any recipe is laughter! With each recipe, you'll also find a fun fact and a silly joke.

Are you ready to make something delicious? Let's go!

Kids in the Kitchen Every Day

The kitchen is my playground. No, there isn't a slide or a swing, but there are bright colors, wonderful smells, and delicious bites. Grab your apron and come join me! We'll have a great time.

KITCHEN RULES

Wonderful things come out of the kitchen: delicious foods, comforting smells, and lots and lots of smiles and laughter. But there are some basic rules you should always follow during food preparation. Parents may also have some rules to add to this list, so be sure to check in with them.

1. **Cook with an adult.** 🛑 ← When you see this symbol, it means an adult needs to supervise or help. Some steps may require a bit more help than others, such as using the stovetop or handling the food processor (sharp!). You might also need a hand when taking something out of the hot oven. Remember, a good chef always accepts help when they need it.

NOTE TO GROWN-UPS

Now is a good time to go over any specific rules you have in your kitchen that may not be mentioned here.

2. **Wash your hands.** The first step in cooking is washing your hands. The second step is to *not* pick your nose. *Yuck!* Whatever is on our hands will get on (and in!) the food, so start with clean hands. Wash them under warm water while singing the "Happy Birthday" song twice. Get soap between those fingers and clean under those nails, too. Squeaky clean is the name of the game.

3. **Wash fruits and vegetables.** Fruits and veggies were in the soil, then on a truck, then in the supermarket before making their way to your kitchen counter. Even if you're peeling something, it's best to wash it well anyway. Water is usually good enough, but to be extra clean, break out a veggie scrubber and go to town.

4. **Handle eggs and meat safely.** Some raw foods are safer to handle than others. If you're using eggs or raw meat, be sure to start with clean hands and a clean work area. Wash your hands right away after touching egg or raw meat. Afterward, clean your cutting board and work area *really* well before putting anything else down on that spot. Make sure you have a cutting board that's only for meat. Use a different cutting board for everything else.

5. **Prepare your work area.** Wipe down your work area with a clean, damp cloth before starting to cook. Also, make sure you have enough open space to work. You should stand at a height that brings your belly to the same height as your work area. If you don't have a learning tower or other safe way to get up to the height of the counter, create a workplace on the floor. Spread out a clean blanket or towel, and set up your tools and ingredients.

6. **Clean as you go.** You're going to want a bite of your delicious creation as soon as it's ready. Clean your tools and equipment as you go so you don't have a pile of dirty dishes in the sink waiting for you. If something is in the oven, or the dough is resting, or your tasty dish is cooling down, wash some dishes to pass the time.

COMMON COOKING TOOLS

You don't need many tools to prepare something tasty. The tools listed here are some you will reach for again and again. They will become as familiar as that favorite bedtime book.

TOOLS & UTENSILS

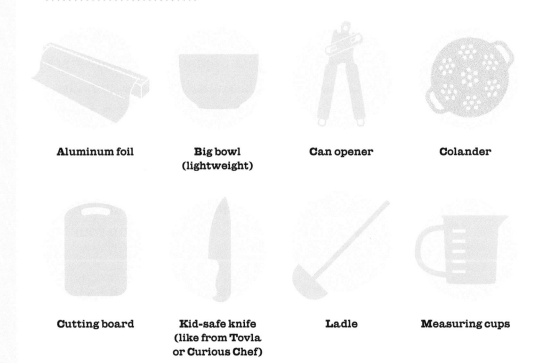

Aluminum foil

Big bowl
(lightweight)

Can opener

Colander

Cutting board

Kid-safe knife
(like from Tovla
or Curious Chef)

Ladle

Measuring cups

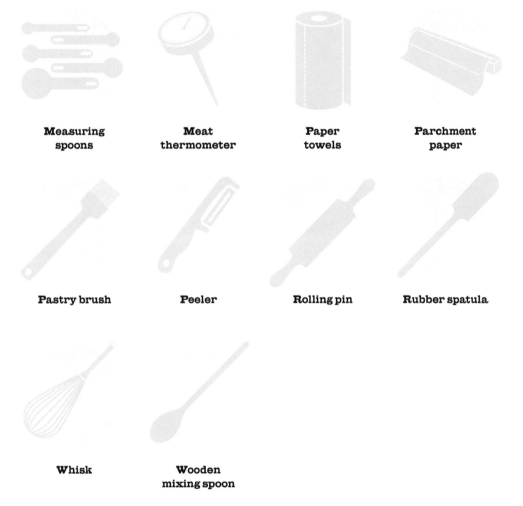

Measuring
spoons

Meat
thermometer

Paper
towels

Parchment
paper

Pastry brush

Peeler

Rolling pin

Rubber spatula

Whisk

Wooden
mixing spoon

COOKWARE & BAKEWARE

12-cup muffin pan   **Baking sheet (rimmed)**   **Frying pan**   **Lasagna pan**

Mixing bowls (small, medium, and large)   **Roasting pan**   **Soup pot**

APPLIANCES

Blender (stand or immersion)   **Food processor**   **Toaster oven**

BEFORE YOU START

Keep these points in mind as you get ready to cook.

1. **Read the recipe.** Read the *whole* recipe before you begin. Are you going to have to do two steps at the same time? Or let your dough rest? It's best to know before you begin.

2. **Check that you have all the ingredients and tools.** If you realize halfway through the recipe that you're missing something important, like milk, you might have to replace it with hummingbird food, and it might not be very delicious.

3. **Set out all of the ingredients and tools you'll need.** Being organized makes it easier to reach what you need when you need it.

4. **Measure carefully.** When you're first learning how to cook, follow the instructions exactly. It's the best way to learn how ingredients work together.

5. **Always be safe.** Safety is the most important thing—in addition to handwashing and making sure your ingredients and workspace are clean. It also includes picking up the LEGOs off the floor so you don't step on one. (*Ouch!*)

LET'S GET COOKING

You know the rules.
You've got your tools.
Now crack open the book.
And choose something
to cook!

Green Hulk Smoothie *page 10*

Breakfast

Good morning, chefs!
Grab your whisk and get your bowl.
Get ready to rock and get ready to roll!
It's time to make something savory
or sweet.
And when you're the chef, it can't
be beat!

Green Hulk Smoothie

How did the Hulk get his strength? With a cold, delicious Green Hulk Smoothie!

KITCHEN TOOLS YOU WILL NEED

Measuring cup

Colander

Measuring spoon

Blender

INGREDIENTS YOU WILL NEED

1 cup **fresh spinach**

1 cup **whole milk or non-dairy alternative**

2 tablespoons **honey** (or to taste)

1 **frozen banana**

PREP TIME
5 minutes

MAKES
1
SERVING

GLUTEN-FREE
NUT-FREE
VEGETARIAN

DIRECTIONS

1. Rinse the spinach. Place the spinach in the colander and rinse it in the sink. Let it drain before completing step 3.

2. Combine the milk and honey. Pour the milk and honey into the blender.

3. Add the remaining ingredients. Add the banana and spinach to the blender.

4. Blend until completely smooth.

5. Serve. Pour the smoothie into a cup and enjoy!

? DID YOU KNOW?

Medieval artists used spinach to make green paint.

I MADE THIS
RECIPE ON:
(DATE)

IT TASTED:
(CIRCLE
THE STARS)

WHO
HELPED?

JUST FOR
LAUGHS

What's a dancer's favorite kind of vegetable?

Spin–ach!

Waffle Bowl Parfait

Parfait is said like *par-FAY*. It is French for "perfect." Do you think a parfait is perfect?

KITCHEN TOOLS YOU WILL NEED

Kid-safe knife

Cutting board

Measuring cup

Measuring spoon

INGREDIENTS YOU WILL NEED

1 **banana**

4 medium **strawberries**

½ cup plain, full-fat **Greek yogurt**

1 **waffle bowl**

½ cup **blueberries**

1 tablespoon **hulled hemp seeds**

PREP TIME
5 minutes

MAKES
1
SERVING

NUT-FREE
VEGETARIAN

I MADE THIS
RECIPE ON:
(DATE)

- -

IT TASTED:
(CIRCLE
THE STARS)

★ ★ ★ ★ ★

WHO
HELPED?

- -

- -

- -

- -

JUST FOR
LAUGHS

**Who scared
the strawberry?**

The booberry.

DIRECTIONS

1. **Chop the fruit.** Carefully chop the banana and strawberries into bite-size pieces.

2. **Add the yogurt.** Spoon the yogurt into the waffle bowl.

3. **Layer the fruit.** Layer the bananas, strawberries, and blueberries on top.

4. **Top with hemp seeds.** Sprinkle hemp seeds over the fruit and enjoy!

DID YOU KNOW?

Strawberries are the only fruit to wear their seeds on their skin.

Teddy Bear Toast

It's a very beary breakfast when Teddy Bear Toast comes to the table.

PREP TIME
5 minutes

COOK TIME
5 minutes

MAKES
1
SERVING

VEGAN
VEGETARIAN

KITCHEN TOOLS YOU WILL NEED

Toaster

Measuring spoon

Butter knife

Cutting board

Kid-safe knife

INGREDIENTS YOU WILL NEED

1 piece **bread** (use your favorite kind)

2 tablespoons **peanut butter**, **cream cheese**, or other favorite spread

1 **banana**

3 **blueberries or raisins**

 I MADE THIS
RECIPE ON:
(DATE)

 IT TASTED:
(CIRCLE
THE STARS)

★ ★ ★ ★ ★

 WHO
HELPED?

- -

- -

- -

- -

 JUST FOR
LAUGHS

**Why do bananas
never get lonely?**

Because they hang
out in bunches.

DIRECTIONS

1. Make the toast. Toast the bread until golden or light brown.

2. Make the teddy bear's head. Using the butter knife, spread the peanut butter or spread of your choice over the toast, making a large circle for the bear's face and two smaller circles for the bear's ears.

3. Decorate the bear's face. Using the kid-safe knife, cut the banana into rounds. Place one round in each small circle to finish the ears. Place another round in the middle of the large circle to make a nose. Then place 1 blueberry on the nose and 2 blueberries above the nose to make eyes.

4. Enjoy!

? DID YOU KNOW?

Bananas float in water. That's because they are less dense than water.

Yaffi's Super Tasty Scones

Scones have been a delicious breakfast food since the year 1513! Be part of history with this tasty dish.

PREP TIME
15 minutes

COOK TIME
15 minutes

MAKES
16
SCONES

NUT-FREE
VEGETARIAN

KITCHEN TOOLS YOU WILL NEED

Baking sheet

Parchment paper

Large mixing bowl

Measuring cups

Measuring spoons

Mixing spoon

Kid-safe knife

Medium mixing bowl

INGREDIENTS YOU WILL NEED

1 cup **all-purpose flour**

1 cup **whole-wheat flour**

1 tablespoon **white sugar**

2 tablespoons **brown sugar**

1 teaspoon **baking powder**

¼ teaspoon **baking soda**

2 tablespoons **flax meal** (ground flaxseed)

½ cup (1 stick) **salted butter**, cold

½ cup **full-fat sour cream**

¼ teaspoon **pure vanilla extract**

1 **large egg**

⅓ cup **chocolate chips** (use your favorite kind)

I MADE THIS
RECIPE ON:
(DATE)

IT TASTED:
(CIRCLE
THE STARS)

WHO
HELPED?

JUST FOR
LAUGHS

What's a car's
favorite meal?

Brake-fast.

DIRECTIONS

1. 🛑 Preheat* **the oven and prepare the pan.** Preheat the oven to 400°F. Line a baking sheet with parchment paper.

2. **Mix the dry ingredients.** In the large mixing bowl, combine the flours, sugars, baking powder, baking soda, and flax meal. Stir well.

3. **Cut the butter.** Cut the butter into small cubes (the size of the end of your pinkie finger). Add to the bowl of dry ingredients.

4. Smoosh* **the butter.** Using both hands, smoosh the butter into the dry ingredients. Do this until the flour mixture looks and feels like sand (it should take about 5 minutes).

✳ Preheat:
Turning on the oven and setting it to the temperature indicated. Wait until the oven reaches that temperature before you put anything into it (ask an adult to help you).

✳ Smoosh:
Squeezing the flour and butter mixture through your fists over and over until all of the ingredients are well mixed.

5. **Mix the wet ingredients.** In the medium mixing bowl, combine the sour cream, vanilla, and egg. Stir well. Carefully pour the wet ingredients into the dry ingredients. Stir everything together until well incorporated (that means it all looks the same).

6. **Add the chocolate chips.** Pour the chocolate chips into the dough. Using your hands, mix them in until they are evenly distributed.

7. **Shape the scones.** Using both hands, form the dough into a ball, and then press it flat until it's as tall as your thumb (about an inch). Using the knife, cut the flattened circle of dough into 8 even triangles—do this by cutting all the way across the circle (like cutting a pizza) 4 times. Sprinkle sugar on top of the triangles and place them on the prepared baking sheet, spacing them 1 inch apart.

8. 🛑 **Bake.** Place the pan in the preheated oven. Bake for 15 minutes, or until a toothpick inserted in the middle of a scone comes out clean. Let cool on the pan for 15 to 20 minutes.

MAKE IT YOUR OWN

Try swapping the chocolate chips for chopped nuts, cinnamon chips, or something different!

I MADE IT MY OWN BY:

Microwave Muglette

Eggs are a great way to start the day! Consider making this simple breakfast for your parents.

KITCHEN TOOLS YOU WILL NEED

Coffee mug (microwave-safe)

Fork

Measuring spoons

Kid-safe knife

Spoon

INGREDIENTS YOU WILL NEED

Olive oil cooking spray

2 **large eggs**

1 tablespoon **whole milk or non-dairy alternative**

1 tablespoon grated **cheddar cheese**

1 tablespoon finely chopped **broccoli florets**

1 teaspoon finely chopped **green onion**

Pinch **salt** (1/8 teaspoon)

Pinch **freshly ground black pepper** (1/8 teaspoon)

Pinch **garlic powder** (1/8 teaspoon)

I MADE THIS
RECIPE ON:
(DATE)

- - - - - - - - - - - - - - - - - - -

IT TASTED:
(CIRCLE
THE STARS)

★ ★ ★ ★ ★

WHO
HELPED?

- - - - - - - - - - - - - - - - - - -

- - - - - - - - - - - - - - - - - - -

- - - - - - - - - - - - - - - - - - -

JUST FOR
LAUGHS

What does Mr. Egg say every morning to Mrs. Egg?

"Have an eggs-tra special day!"

DIRECTIONS

1. Grease the mug. Lightly spray the inside of the coffee mug with the olive oil.

2. Crack the eggs. Crack the eggs into the greased* mug. Add the milk. Using the fork, beat* the egg mixture until well combined.

3. Chop the veggies. Chop the broccoli and the green onion into very small pieces.

4. Add the cheese and veggies. Add the cheese, broccoli, and green onions to the mug and beat until well combined.

✳ Grease:
Covering the surface of a pan with oil. This helps baked goods slide out of the pan easily once cooked.

✳ Beat:
Stirring really fast to thoroughly combine ingredients and add air, helping to make baked items light and fluffy.

5. **Add the spices.** Sprinkle in the salt, pepper, and garlic powder and mix well.

6. **Microwave.** Place the mug into the microwave and heat for 30 seconds. STOP Take the mug out and stir. Return the mug to the microwave and heat for another 30 seconds, then take the mug out and stir. Repeat this step, heating for 30 seconds and stirring, until the eggs are set and firm.

7. **Enjoy!** Eat right out of the cup or turn the mug over onto a plate. (The eggs will slide right out.)

MAKE IT
YOUR OWN

Change up the veggies. Swap out the broccoli for chopped bell pepper, spinach, or zucchini.

I MADE IT MY OWN BY:

Slow Cooker Lentil Soup *page 30*

3

Soups & Savory Snacks

Soups and snacks to warm your belly.
Crackers crunch, all dipped in jelly.
Food gives you energy and makes
you smile.
And when you're the chef, you can do
it in style!

Slow Cooker Lentil Soup

Lentil soup is popular all over the world. Want to find out why? Just taste it.

KITCHEN TOOLS YOU WILL NEED

Peeler

Cutting board

Kid-safe knife

Measuring cup

Slow cooker

Ladle

INGREDIENTS YOU WILL NEED

2 large **carrots**

1 stalk **celery**

1 large **onion**

1 (16-ounce) bag **dried brown lentils**, rinsed and drained

8 cups **vegetable stock**

1 (15.5-ounce) can **fire-roasted diced tomatoes**

½ teaspoon **salt**

¼ teaspoon **freshly ground black pepper**

2 cups lightly packed **fresh spinach**

PREP TIME
10 minutes

COOK TIME
6 hours

MAKES
6
SERVINGS

DAIRY-FREE
GLUTEN-FREE
NUT-FREE
VEGAN
VEGETARIAN

DIRECTIONS

1. Prepare the veggies. Peel and slice the carrots. Slice the celery. Dice the onion. Chop the spinach.

2. Dump it in! Add the chopped carrots, celery, and onion to the slow cooker. Then add the lentils, stock, tomatoes, salt, and pepper to the slow cooker, too. Cover with the lid and cook on Low for 6 hours.

3. Spinach your bowl. Add ⅓ cup spinach to the bottom of each soup bowl. (STOP) Ladle the soup over the spinach. Enjoy!

I MADE THIS RECIPE ON:
(DATE)

IT TASTED:
(CIRCLE THE STARS)

★ ★ ★ ★ ★

WHO HELPED?

JUST FOR LAUGHS

What do you get when you spill soup on a comic book?

Souperman.

Cucumber Cups with Tuna Salad

This dish is perfect for picnics—you eat the container!

PREP TIME
15 minutes

MAKES
2
SERVINGS

DAIRY-FREE
GLUTEN-FREE
NUT-FREE

KITCHEN TOOLS YOU WILL NEED

Peeler

Kid-safe knife

Cutting board

Teaspoon

Can opener

Medium mixing bowl

Measuring spoons

Cookie cutter (if you want to cut the cucumber into fun shapes)

INGREDIENTS YOU WILL NEED

1 large **English cucumber**

1 (5-ounce) can chunk light **tuna**

3 tablespoons **mayonnaise**

1 teaspoon **sweet pickle relish**

1 teaspoon **fresh lemon juice**

I MADE THIS
RECIPE ON:
(DATE)

- - - - - - - - - - - - - - - - - - - -

IT TASTED:
(CIRCLE
THE STARS)

★ ★ ★ ★ ★

WHO
HELPED?

- - - - - - - - - - - - - - - - - - - -

- - - - - - - - - - - - - - - - - - - -

- - - - - - - - - - - - - - - - - - - -

JUST FOR
LAUGHS

**Why are cats afraid
of cucumbers?**

They don't like
anything cooler
than they are.

DIRECTIONS

1. Peel the cucumber. Using the peeler, remove the skin from the cucumber. If your cucumber has a thinner, sweeter skin, you can leave it on.

2. Make the cups. Cut the peeled cucumber into thumb-size lengths, about 2 inches thick. Cut an X into the top of each cucumber piece, into the seeds, leaving the edges of the cucumber whole.

3. Scoop out the seeds. Using the teaspoon, carefully scoop the seeds out of each cucumber piece to make a little cup.

4. **Prepare the filling.** (STOP) Open the can of tuna. Squeeze the extra liquid out of the tuna. In the medium mixing bowl, stir together the tuna, mayonnaise, relish, and lemon juice.

5. **Fill your cup.** Using the same spoon from Step 3, fill your cucumber cups with tuna salad. Enjoy!

DID YOU KNOW?

Cucumbers were first grown domestically in ancient India.

Veggie Skeleton with Hummus

What could make your hummus more boo-tiful than this fun skeleton? Learn anatomy at snack time!

PREP TIME
15 minutes

MAKES 1 SKELETON (ENOUGH FOR 2 PEOPLE)

DAIRY-FREE
GLUTEN-FREE
NUT-FREE
VEGAN
VEGETARIAN

KITCHEN TOOLS YOU WILL NEED

Kid-safe knife

Cutting board

Platter or serving plate

Measuring cup

INGREDIENTS YOU WILL NEED

1 **bell pepper** (any color), cored and sliced lengthwise

1 head **cauliflower,** cut into florets

1 head **broccoli,** cut into florets

1 **mushroom**

2 **cherry tomatoes**

10 **green beans**

1 **carrot**

1 cup **hummus**

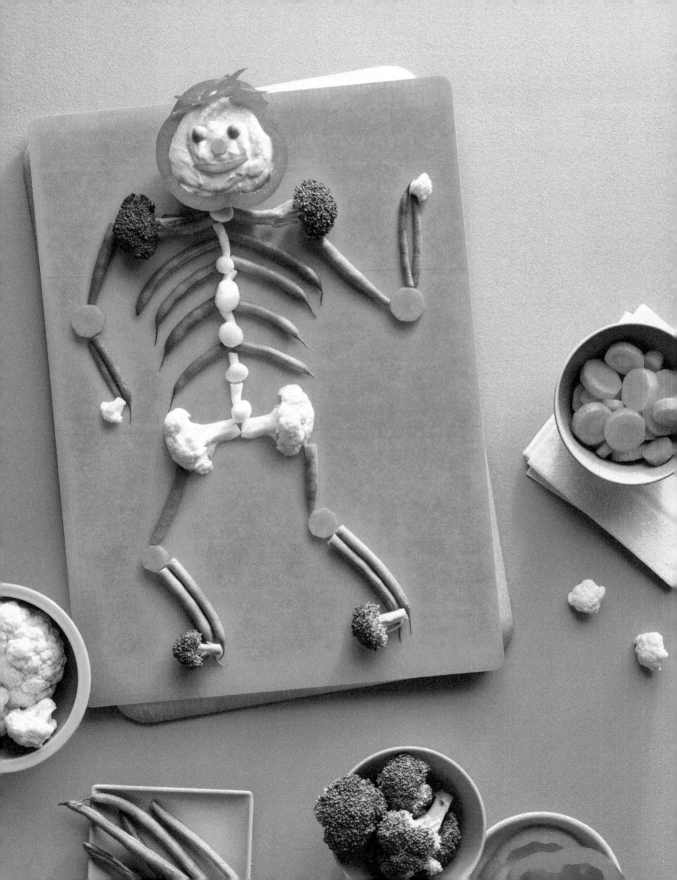

 I MADE THIS
RECIPE ON:
(DATE)

 IT TASTED:
(CIRCLE
THE STARS)

★ ★ ★ ★ ★

 WHO
HELPED?

- -

- -

- -

- -

 JUST FOR
LAUGHS

**Why wouldn't
the skeleton
go skydiving?**

He didn't have the
guts for it.

DIRECTIONS

1. Prepare the veggies. Cut a ring out of your bell pepper by placing the pepper on its side and cutting down toward the cutting board two times. Remove the seeds. Next, cut the cauliflower into florets. Do the same with the broccoli. Cut the mushroom and cherry tomatoes in half. Cut the carrot into rounds.

2. **Build the skeleton's body.** On a platter or serving plate, make a skeleton body using the pieces of vegetables. Use the bell pepper ring as the head.

3. **Fill the head.** Fill your skeleton's head with hummus. Enjoy!

MAKE IT YOUR OWN

Get creative with your dip! Guacamole adds a creepy sheen to your new favorite bony friend. Queso adds a delicious kick. What other dips could you try?

I MADE IT MY OWN BY:

DID YOU KNOW?

The smallest bone in your body is in your ear. The longest bone is in your leg.

Crispy Baked Taquitos

Nothing satisfies like the crunch of taquitos, except maybe making them yourself.

PREP TIME
10 minutes

COOK TIME
30 minutes

MAKES
12
TAQUITOS

GLUTEN-FREE
NUT-FREE
VEGETARIAN

KITCHEN TOOLS YOU WILL NEED

Baking sheet

Aluminum foil

Medium mixing bowl

Measuring cup

Measuring spoons

Potato masher

Paper towels

INGREDIENTS YOU WILL NEED

Olive oil cooking spray

½ cup cooked **pinto beans**, drained and rinsed

1 teaspoon **ground cumin**

¼ teaspoon **garlic powder**

¼ teaspoon **onion powder**

½ teaspoon **kosher salt**

1 cup **shredded cheddar cheese**

½ cup **frozen corn kernels**, thawed

12 **corn tortillas**

I MADE THIS
RECIPE ON:
(DATE)

IT TASTED:
(CIRCLE
THE STARS)

★ ★ ★ ★ ★

WHO
HELPED?

JUST FOR
LAUGHS

Did you see this week's forecast?

It's gonna be cold today, hot tamale.

DIRECTIONS

1. 🛑 **Preheat the oven and prepare the pan.** Preheat the oven to 400°F. Line the baking sheet with aluminum foil, then spray it lightly with the olive oil.

2. **Prepare the filling.** In the medium bowl, combine the beans, cumin, garlic powder, onion powder, and salt. Using the potato masher, mash the beans until the ingredients are all mixed together.

3. **Add the cheese and corn.** Stir in the shredded cheese and corn. Stir well.

4. **Soften the tortillas.** Place 2 corn tortillas between two damp paper towel sheets. Place in the microwave and heat for 20 seconds. (This will help the tortillas roll up nicely.)

5. **Stuff and roll.** (STOP) Remove the warm tortillas from the microwave. Spread 2 tablespoons of the bean mixture onto one half of each softened tortilla, placing the mixture on the side of the tortilla closest to your tummy. Roll them up and place seam-side down on the prepared baking sheet. Spray the tortillas with the olive oil. Repeat steps 4 and 5 for the remaining 10 tortillas.

6. **Bake.** (STOP) Place the pan into the preheated oven. Bake for 25 minutes until golden and crunchy. Remove the pan from the oven and let cool for 5 minutes before eating. Enjoy!

MAKE IT YOUR OWN

Change up the filling or pair it with a delicious dip! What do you think would taste better: sour cream, guacamole, or queso? What other kinds of beans could you use in the filling?

I MADE IT MY OWN BY:

....

....

....

....

....

Toasted Za'atar Crackers

Crackers are delicious. But did you know you can make your own? Try these with hummus or another tasty dip.

PREP TIME
15 minutes
COOK TIME
35 minutes

MAKES ABOUT
40
CRACKERS

DAIRY-FREE
GLUTEN-FREE
VEGAN
VEGETARIAN

KITCHEN TOOLS YOU WILL NEED

Medium bowl

Measuring cup

Measuring spoons

Mixing spoon

Parchment paper

Rolling pin

Pizza slicer

INGREDIENTS YOU WILL NEED

1 cup **almond flour** (not almond meal)

1 tablespoon **ground flaxseed**

½ teaspoon **kosher salt**

3 tablespoons **water**

1 tablespoon **za'atar seasoning**

 I MADE THIS
RECIPE ON:
(DATE)

- -

 IT TASTED:
(CIRCLE
THE STARS)

★ ★ ★ ★ ★

 WHO
HELPED?

- -

- -

- -

 JUST FOR
LAUGHS

Why do sharks only swim in salt water?

Because pepper water makes them sneeze!

DIRECTIONS

1. (STOP) **Preheat the oven to 350°F.**

2. **Prepare the dough.** In the medium bowl, combine the almond flour, flaxseed, salt, and water. Stir together until it forms a dough.

3. **Roll the dough.** Place the dough between two large sheets of parchment paper. Using your hands, spread it out as much as you can. Then, with a rolling pin, roll out the dough until it's about as thick as the end of your pinkie finger, about ⅛ inch. Try to shape it into a rectangle. It's okay if it's not perfect.

4. **Season.** Remove the top piece of parchment paper. Sprinkle the za'atar seasoning over the whole rectangle of dough. Using the rolling pin, press the seasoning into the dough.

5. **Cut the dough.** Using the pizza slicer, cut the dough into crackers, about 1 inch by 1 inch.

6. **Bake.** (STOP) Keeping it on the parchment paper, transfer the dough into the pre-heated oven. Bake for 25 minutes or until golden. Some of the crackers on the edge might burn a little—that's okay!

7. **Let cool.** (STOP) Carefully remove the parchment paper from the oven. Let the crackers cool for 10 minutes. Enjoy!

MAKE IT YOUR OWN

What kind of seasoning blend will you try next? Coarse salt? Cinnamon and sugar? Everything bagel seasoning? The opportunities are endless.

I MADE IT MY OWN BY:

....

....

....

....

....

Broccoli Potato Cheese Soup

Delicious, warm soup is like a hug for your belly, especially on a cold day.

PREP TIME
10 minutes

COOK TIME
25 minutes

MAKES
6
SERVINGS

GLUTEN-FREE
NUT-FREE

KITCHEN TOOLS YOU WILL NEED

Peeler

Cutting board

Kid-safe knife

Medium saucepan

Measuring spoon

Measuring cup

Wooden stirring spoon

Immersion or stand blender

INGREDIENTS YOU WILL NEED

1 medium head **broccoli** (with stem)

1 large **russet potato**

½ **onion**

1 clove **garlic**

2 tablespoons **olive oil**

4 cups **chicken or vegetable broth**

2 cups **shredded cheddar cheese**

Salt

Freshly ground black pepper

JUST FOR LAUGHS

What kind of music does broccoli listen to?

Broc and Roll!

DIRECTIONS

1. Prepare the veggies. Separate the broccoli stem from the florets. Peel the stem and chop into pieces. Cut the florets into small pieces. Peel and roughly chop the potato. Roughly chop the onion. Mince* the garlic.

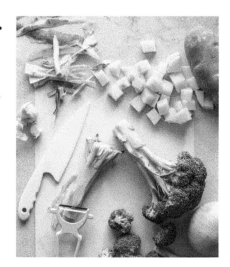

2. (STOP) **Heat the oil.** In the medium saucepan over medium heat, heat the oil until it shimmers.

3. Add the onion and garlic. Add the onion and garlic to the pan, and cook for 3 to 4 minutes, until the onion begins to soften.

4. Add the broth. Pour the broth into the pot and bring to a boil.*

❋ **Mince:** Chopping something into very small pieces.

❋ **Boil:** Heating water to a point where bubbles are quickly rising to the surface.

5. **Add the broccoli stem and potato.** Add the chopped broccoli stem and potato to the pot. Reduce the heat to medium-low and let the soup simmer for 15 minutes or until the potatoes are tender.

6. **Add the cheese.** Stir the cheese into the soup until melted.

7. 🛑 **Blend the soup.** Using an immersion or stand blender, blend the soup until smooth. Alternatively, let the soup cool for 10 minutes, transfer to a standard blender, and blend until smooth.

8. **Season the soup.** Taste the soup and add salt and pepper, as needed.

9. **Add the broccoli florets.** Add the broccoli florets to the blended soup and cook until tender, about 5 minutes.

MAKE IT YOUR OWN

Can you add a topping to make this soup crunchy? Or add another vegetable to the soup?

I MADE IT MY OWN BY:

....

....

....

....

....

DID YOU KNOW?

Queen Victoria was given a giant wheel of cheese weighing 450 kilograms (1,000 pounds) as a wedding gift.

Lavash Sandwich Roll-Up *page 54*

Main Meals

It's dinner time!
Roll and mix and chop and crunch.
It's almost nearly time to munch!
Layer, bake, and giggle, too.
I'm ready to cook! How about you?

Lavash Sandwich Roll-Up

Want to take
your sandwich
to the next level?
Roll it up!

PREP TIME
10 minutes

MAKES
2
SERVINGS

DAIRY-FREE
GLUTEN-FREE
VEGAN
VEGETARIAN

KITCHEN TOOLS YOU WILL NEED

Cutting board

Kid-safe knife

Measuring cup

INGREDIENTS YOU WILL NEED

½ medium **apple** (your favorite kind)

1 **lavash flatbread** (or tortilla, naan, pita, or other flatbread)

¼ cup **nut or seed butter** (your favorite kind)

¼ cup chopped **raisins or dried cranberries**

¼ cup **toasted sunflower seeds**

¼ cup **Cheerios** (or other cereal of your choice)

Pinch ground **cinnamon**

DIRECTIONS

1. **Prepare the apple.** Cut the apple in half and remove the core. Then cut the apple into matchsticks.

2. **Spread the bread.** Lay out the flatbread and spread nut or seed butter over the whole surface.

3. **Add the toppings.** Place the apple matchsticks, lengthwise, down the center of the prepared lavash. Sprinkle the raisins, seeds, and cereal on top of the apples. Dust with the cinnamon.

4. **Roll it up.** Roll up the lavash, lengthwise. Cut the roll in half.

5. **Time to eat!** Serve immediately, or wrap tightly in plastic wrap and refrigerate for a snack later.

I MADE THIS
RECIPE ON:
(DATE)

IT TASTED:
(CIRCLE
THE STARS)

WHO
HELPED?

JUST FOR
LAUGHS

What did the apple say to the walnut?

You're nuts.

? DID YOU KNOW?

In ancient Egypt, cinnamon was so prized that it was valued more than gold!

Roasted Tofu with Broccoli

Tofu doesn't have much taste on its own—it's all in the sauce. Ready for something delicious?

PREP TIME
20 minutes

COOK TIME
40 minutes

MAKES
3
SERVINGS

DAIRY-FREE
NUT-FREE
VEGAN
VEGETARIAN

KITCHEN TOOLS YOU WILL NEED

Baking sheet

Aluminum foil

Measuring spoons

Tofu press (or two large plates and a heavy book)

2 medium bowls

Mixing spoon

Large bowl

Kid-safe knife

Cutting board

Pastry brush

Cookie cutter (if you want to cut the tofu into fun shapes)

INGREDIENTS YOU WILL NEED

3 tablespoons **olive oil**, divided

3 tablespoons **brown sugar**

1 tablespoon **sesame oil**

2 tablespoons **soy sauce** (or coconut aminos, to make it gluten-free)

2 cloves **garlic**, diced

¼ teaspoon **ground ginger** or ½ teaspoon grated fresh ginger

1 (16-ounce) block **firm tofu**

16 ounces **broccoli florets**

Pinch **kosher salt**

I MADE THIS
RECIPE ON:
(DATE)

- - - - - - - - - - - - - - - -

IT TASTED:
(CIRCLE
THE STARS)

★ ★ ★ ★ ★

WHO
HELPED?

- - - - - - - - - - - - - - - -

- - - - - - - - - - - - - - - -

- - - - - - - - - - - - - - - -

DIRECTIONS

1. (STOP) **Preheat the oven and prepare the pan.**
Preheat the oven to 425°F. Line the baking sheet with aluminum foil. Lightly coat the foil with 1 tablespoon of olive oil.

2. Press * the tofu.
Set a large plate on the counter and place the tofu on it. Add another plate, upside down, on top of the tofu. Carefully balance a book on top of the plate. Set it aside for 10 minutes.

* **Press:**
Placing tofu between two hard surfaces to press out the water—this makes the tofu suck up more marinade so it's more flavorful.

* **Marinade:**
A sauce that an ingredient is soaked in to add flavor.

3. Make the marinade.✳ In one medium bowl, combine the sugar, sesame oil, soy sauce, garlic, and ginger. Stir well. Pour half of the marinade into the large bowl (and save the rest of the sauce for dipping). Add the pressed tofu to the large bowl. Let the tofu marinate while you continue with the recipe.

4. Toss✳ **the broccoli.** Okay, not literally! In the other medium bowl, combine the broccoli with the remaining 2 tablespoons of olive oil and the salt. Set aside.

5. Bake. (STOP) Spread the marinated tofu in a single layer on the prepared baking sheet and place the pan in the oven. Bake for 10 minutes on one side. Carefully remove the pan from the oven. Flip the tofu over. Add the broccoli florets to the pan, arranging them around the tofu. Bake for another 10 minutes, until the tofu begins to shrink. Remove the pan from the oven. Let cool for 10 minutes before serving. Enjoy!

✳ **Toss:**
Combining ingredients by using a gentle lifting motion.

DID YOU KNOW?

The process of making tofu is very close to the process of making cheese! Both require coagulation, or thickening, of milk—soy milk in this case.

Scrumptious Spinach Lasagna

Who doesn't love a good lasagna? It's noodles, sauce, and cheese—the makings of a perfect dinner.

PREP TIME
10 minutes

COOK TIME
1 hour
20 minutes

MAKES
12
SERVINGS

NUT-FREE
VEGETARIAN

KITCHEN TOOLS YOU WILL NEED

9-by-13-inch baking pan

Mixing bowl

Measuring spoon

Mixing spoon

Pastry brush

Measuring cup

Parchment paper

INGREDIENTS YOU WILL NEED

Olive oil cooking spray

10 ounces **frozen chopped spinach**, thawed

15 ounces **ricotta cheese**

2 teaspoons minced **garlic**

1 (24-ounce) jar **marinara sauce**

12 ounces oven-ready **lasagna noodles**

2½ cups **shredded mozzarella cheese**, divided

 **I MADE THIS RECIPE ON:**
(DATE)

- - - - - - - - - - - - - - - - - -

 **IT TASTED:**
(CIRCLE THE STARS)

 **WHO HELPED?**

- - - - - - - - - - - - - - - - - -

- - - - - - - - - - - - - - - - - -

- - - - - - - - - - - - - - - - - -

 **JUST FOR LAUGHS**

A father says to his son while eating Lasagna, "Lean over your plate."
The boy asks, "Why?"

"So you'll get less-on-ya."

DIRECTIONS:

1. 🛑 **Preheat the oven and prepare the pan.** Preheat the oven to 375°F. Spray the baking pan on all sides with the olive oil.

2. Prepare the spinach. Unwrap the spinach and squeeze out the excess liquid. (You can do this with a colander* or just using your hands.)

3. Make the filling. In the mixing bowl, combine the spinach, ricotta, and garlic. Stir well.

4. Start stacking the noodles. Cover the bottom of the prepared baking pan with a thin layer of marinara sauce. Lay a single layer of lasagna noodles on top.

5. Continue layering the noodles. Using the pastry brush, brush marinara on top of the noodles. Then spread 1 cup of the ricotta-spinach mixture evenly over the noodles. Sprinkle ½ cup of the mozzarella on top.

✳ **Colander:**
A bowl-shaped instrument with many holes used for draining food.

6. Repeat. Cover your creation with another single layer of lasagna noodles. Repeat, adding marinara, filling, and noodles until you've reached the top of your baking dish (finish with a layer of noodles—you should have 4 layers in total).

7. Finish. Brush the top layer of noodles with marinara. Cover with the remaining mozzarella.

8. Bake. (STOP) Cover the dish with parchment paper. Bake in the preheated oven for 50 minutes, until the cheese is melted and the sauce is bubbling. Uncover and bake for 10 more minutes, just until the top is lightly browned.

9. Enjoy. (STOP) Remove the pan from the oven. Let cool for 10 minutes before cutting.

MAKE IT YOUR OWN

What other veggies would be great in lasagna? Is there a different sauce you would like to try?

I MADE IT MY OWN BY:

DID YOU KNOW?

The word "lasagna" didn't originally refer to a food. It was the pot that the food was cooked in! It's possible that the word for the pot came from the Greek word meaning "chamber pot" (a bowl used to go to the bathroom in!).

Slow Cooker Vegetable Chili

Nothing warms your tummy like a bowl of chili. Top this one with sour cream and cheese.

PREP TIME
20 minutes

COOK TIME
6 to 8 hours

MAKES
10
SERVINGS

**NUT-FREE
VEGETARIAN**

KITCHEN TOOLS YOU WILL NEED

Swimming goggles

Kid-safe knife

Cutting board

Large skillet

Measuring cup

Slow cooker

Can opener

Measuring spoons

Wooden spoon

INGREDIENTS YOU WILL NEED

2 **bell peppers** (color of choice)

2 stalks **celery**

2 **yellow onions**

2 cloves **garlic**

¼ cup **olive oil**

1 (15.5-ounce) can **black beans**, rinsed and drained

1 (16-ounce) can **kidney beans**, rinsed and drained

1 (14.5-ounce) can **diced tomatoes**

3 tablespoons **chili powder**

1 tablespoon **dried oregano** or 3 tablespoons fresh oregano

1 teaspoon **salt**

1 teaspoon **ground cumin**

¼ teaspoon **freshly ground black pepper**

1 tablespoon **distilled white vinegar**

Sour cream, for topping (optional)

Cheese of your choice, for topping (optional)

I MADE THIS
RECIPE ON:
(DATE)

- - - - - - - - - - - - - - - - -

IT TASTED:
(CIRCLE
THE STARS)

WHO
HELPED?

- - - - - - - - - - - - - - - - -

- - - - - - - - - - - - - - - - -

- - - - - - - - - - - - - - - - -

- - - - - - - - - - - - - - - - -

DIRECTIONS

1. Prepare the vegetables. Put on your swimming goggles (trust me on this). Chop the bell peppers (remove seeds), celery, onions, and garlic. (You can remove the goggles now, if you like.)

2. Sauté* **the onions and garlic.** 🛑 Heat a large skillet over medium-high heat. Carefully pour in the olive oil. Then add the onions and garlic. Sauté until the onions become clear, about 5 minutes.

3. Sauté the celery and bell pepper. 🛑 Add the celery and bell pepper to the skillet with the onions and garlic. Sauté for another 5 minutes, until soft.

4. Place the vegetables in the slow cooker. Transfer the sautéed vegetables to the bowl of the slow cooker.

✳ Sauté:
Frying food in a small amount of fat (butter or oil, for example) in a shallow pan.

5. Add the remaining ingredients. To the vegetable mixture, add the beans, tomatoes, chili powder, oregano, salt, cumin, black pepper, and vinegar. Stir well with the wooden spoon. Cover with the lid. Cook on Low for 6 to 8 hours. Serve topped with the sour cream and cheese, if using.

? DID YOU KNOW?

Bell peppers go by many names around the world. In the United States, Canada, India, and Malaysia, they're *bell peppers*. In Australia and New Zealand, they are called *capsicum*. In the United Kingdom, they are called simply *peppers*. In Japan, they are *papurika*.

MAKE IT YOUR OWN

Some people love this chili served inside a baked sweet potato—how else could you make this even more delicious?

I MADE IT MY OWN BY:

Homemade Spinach Ravioli

Ravioli is like a delicious little treasure box. Each bite is a mix of textures and flavors.

PREP TIME
40 minutes

COOK TIME
5 minutes

MAKES
6
SERVINGS

NUT-FREE
VEGETARIAN

KITCHEN TOOLS YOU WILL NEED

Large mixing bowl

Measuring cup

Measuring spoons

Wooden spoon

Kid-safe knife

Kitchen towel

Food processor or blender

Rolling pin or pasta press

2-inch round cookie cutter or cup with a thin lid

Teaspoon

Fork

Large pot

INGREDIENTS YOU WILL NEED

1 cup **semolina flour**

½ cup **whole-wheat flour**

½ cup **water**

2 tablespoons **olive oil**

½ teaspoon **kosher salt**

16 ounces **ricotta cheese**

2 cups **fresh spinach**

2 teaspoons **minced garlic**

1 teaspoon **dried oregano**

2 to 3 **fresh basil leaves**

1 (24-ounce) jar of **marinara sauce** (or your favorite pasta sauce)

I MADE THIS
RECIPE ON:
(DATE)

....

IT TASTED:
(CIRCLE
THE STARS)

★ ★ ★ ★ ★

WHO
HELPED?

JUST FOR
LAUGHS

**What do you call
pasta with a cold?**

Macaroni and sneeze.

DIRECTIONS

1. **Make the dough.** In the large mixing bowl, combine the flours, water, olive oil, and salt. Using the wooden spoon, stir the dough until a ball forms, about 3 minutes.

2. Knead✳ **the dough.** Turn the dough out onto a clean, floured work surface. Knead the dough until it seems stretchy, about 10 minutes. Using your hands, shape the dough into a neat circle. Next, cut the dough ball into 3 or 4 even portions. Set aside and cover with a kitchen towel.

3. **Make the filling.** In the bowl of the food processor or blender, combine the ricotta, spinach, garlic, oregano, and basil. Pulse until the ingredients are fully incorporated.

✳ Knead:
Mixing dough by stretching, pulling, and pushing.

4. Roll out the dough and cut out ravioli. `STOP` Take one portion of dough and, using the rolling pin, roll it out until paper thin, about ⅛ inch thick. Using the cookie cutter or cup, cut the dough into circles. Gather up the scraps and repeat, rolling and cutting until you have used up as much of the dough as you can.

5. Fill the ravioli. Set half of the dough rounds aside to use as lids. With the remaining rounds, spoon 1 teaspoon of the prepared filling in the center of each dough round, leaving a border for pinching the ravioli shut (if your rounds are bigger, you'll use more filling). Top each filled round with the saved pasta "lids." Using a fork, press down on the sides to seal the ravioli shut.

6. Cook the ravioli. `STOP` Bring the large pot filled with water to a boil. Add a pinch of salt to the boiling water. Carefully drop in the ravioli. Cook until they float to the surface, 2 to 3 minutes.

7. Enjoy. Serve with the marinara or your favorite sauce.

MAKE IT YOUR OWN

Want to try a different filling? Or a different sauce? How about a lovely green pesto or a creamy Alfredo?

I MADE IT MY OWN BY:

....

....

....

....

....

Simple Roasted Chicken with Sweet Potatoes

Impress your parents and friends with this easy but fancy dinner.

KITCHEN TOOLS YOU WILL NEED

Swimming goggles

Kid-safe knife

Cutting board

Peeler

Dutch oven or roasting pan

Small mixing bowl

Measuring spoons

Measuring cups

Meat thermometer

INGREDIENTS YOU WILL NEED

2 **yellow onions**

3 large **sweet potatoes**

Olive oil cooking spray

Whole chicken (skin-on, bone-in), cut into 8 pieces (about 3 pounds)

Pinch **kosher salt**

¼ teaspoon **freshly ground black pepper**

1 teaspoon **sweet paprika**

1½ teaspoons **minced garlic**

½ cup **honey**

½ cup **water**

 I MADE THIS
RECIPE ON:
(DATE)

 IT TASTED:
(CIRCLE
THE STARS)

★ ★ ★ ★ ★

 WHO
HELPED?

JUST FOR
LAUGHS

**How do chickens
wake up in
the morning?**

With an alarm cluck!

1. 🛑 **Preheat the oven to 400°F.**

2. **Prepare the vegetables.** Put on your swimming goggles. Cut the onions into chunks about the size of a finger. Peel the sweet potatoes and cut them into wedges. (You can remove the goggles now, if you like.)

3. **Prepare the chicken.** Spray the roasting pan with the olive oil. Arrange the chicken pieces skin-side up in the pan. Add the prepared onions and sweet potatoes, wedging them around and under the chicken pieces.

4. **Mix the spices.** In the small mixing bowl, combine the salt, pepper, paprika, garlic, and honey. Drizzle the mixture all over the chicken and veggies. Add the water to the bottom of the pan.

5. Roast. ✳ 🛑 Place the pan in the preheated oven and roast, uncovered, for 1 hour and 20 minutes, until the chicken is golden and cooked through (the internal temperature of the chicken should read 165°F when tested with a meat thermometer).

6. Serve. 🛑 Carefully remove the pan from the oven and let the chicken rest for 10 minutes before serving. Enjoy!

✳ **Roast:** Cooking by using dry heat, such as in an oven.

MAKE IT YOUR OWN

Try using butternut squash instead of sweet potatoes. What might you use instead of chicken?

I MADE IT MY OWN BY:

- - - - - - - - - - - - - - - - - - -

- - - - - - - - - - - - - - - - - - -

- - - - - - - - - - - - - - - - - - -

- - - - - - - - - - - - - - - - - - -

- - - - - - - - - - - - - - - - - - -

One Sheet Chicken Fajitas

A delicious
dinner is only
a few steps
away with these
fajitas! How
do you even
say that word?
Fah-HEE-tas!

PREP TIME
10 minutes

COOK TIME
30 minutes

MAKES
4
SERVINGS

NUT-FREE

KITCHEN TOOLS YOU WILL NEED

Baking sheet

Aluminum foil

Kid-safe knife

Cutting board

Mixing bowl

Measuring spoons

Meat thermometer

INGREDIENTS YOU WILL NEED

Olive oil cooking spray

1½ pounds boneless,
skinless **chicken breasts**

3 **bell peppers**
(any color)

1 small **red onion**

3 teaspoons
taco seasoning

1 teaspoon **kosher salt**

1½ tablespoons **olive oil**

8 small **tortillas** (corn
or flour)

 I MADE THIS
RECIPE ON:
(DATE)

- -

 IT TASTED:
(CIRCLE
THE STARS)

 WHO
HELPED?

- -

- -

- -

- -

 JUST FOR
LAUGHS

What's white, round, and giggles?

A tickled onion.

DIRECTIONS

1. 🛑 **Preheat the oven and prepare the baking sheet.** Preheat the oven to 425°F. Line the baking sheet with aluminum foil. Spray the foil with the olive oil.

2. Prepare the ingredients. Cut the chicken into strips about ½ inch thick. Place in the mixing bowl. Cut the bell peppers into ¼-inch-thick strips. Cut the onion into ¼-inch-thick strips. Place the cut vegetables into the mixing bowl.

3. Season the filling. To the bowl of chicken, add the taco seasoning, salt, and olive oil. Stir well.

4. **Bake.** Spread the chicken and veggie mixture in a single layer on the prepared baking sheet. (STOP) Place the sheet in the oven and bake for 20 minutes, until the chicken is cooked through (the chicken should reach a temperature of 160°F when tested with a meat thermometer).

5. **Enjoy.** (STOP) Remove the pan from the oven. Let cool for 10 minutes before eating. Enjoy with the tortillas.

MAKE IT YOUR OWN

I like to top my fajitas with sour cream, cheese, jalapeños, black beans, and salsa. What kind of delicious mountain will you create?

I MADE IT MY OWN BY:

. . . .

. . . .

. . . .

. . . .

. . . .

Tomato Basil Blender Soup with Baked Grilled Cheese

Grilled cheese and tomato soup is a classic for a reason— it's delicious!

PREP TIME
10 minutes

COOK TIME
30 minutes

MAKES
4
SERVINGS

GLUTEN-FREE
NUT-FREE
VEGETARIAN

KITCHEN TOOLS YOU WILL NEED

Baking sheet

Aluminum foil

Swimming goggles

Kid-safe knife

Cutting board

Medium mixing bowl

Mixing spoons

Blender

INGREDIENTS YOU WILL NEED

Olive oil cooking spray

8 to 10 medium **tomatoes**

2 medium **sweet onions**

4 cloves **garlic**

⅓ cup sliced **fresh basil leaves**

1 teaspoon **salt**

½ teaspoon **freshly ground black pepper**

2 to 3 tablespoons **olive oil**

1 tablespoon **tomato paste**

1 teaspoon **white sugar**

1 tablespoon **salted butter**, divided

4 pieces **bread** (your favorite kind)

4 slices **American cheese** (or preferred alternative)

I MADE THIS
RECIPE ON:
(DATE)

....

IT TASTED:
(CIRCLE
THE STARS)

★ ★ ★ ★ ★

WHO
HELPED?

....

....

....

JUST FOR
LAUGHS

DIRECTIONS

1. ⛔ **Preheat the oven and prepare the pan.** Preheat the oven to 400°F. Line the baking sheet with aluminum foil. Spray the foil with the olive oil.

2. Prepare the veggies. Put on your swimming goggles. Cut the tomatoes into quarters. Slice the onions. Peel the outer flaky skin off the garlic cloves. Place everything into the mixing bowl. (You can remove the goggles now, if you like.)

3. Season the veggies. Add the basil, salt, pepper, and olive oil to the bowl. Stir well. Arrange the prepared veggies in a single layer on the prepared baking sheet.

4. Roast. ⛔ Place the pan into the preheated oven. Bake for 30 minutes, until the veggies are tender and slightly browned.

5. Prepare the grilled cheese. Meanwhile, divide the butter into 4 equal parts and spread each on a piece of bread. Top the buttered bread with a single slice of cheese.

6. **Toast.** (STOP) Place all 4 pieces of bread with cheese directly into a toaster oven or convection oven. Toast for 4 minutes, until the cheese is melted. Carefully remove the cheesy toast from the hot oven. Make a cheesy hug by placing one piece of cheesy toast facedown onto another so the cheese meets in the middle.

7. **Make the soup.** (STOP) Remove the roasted veggies from the oven. Transfer the vegetables to the blender with the tomato paste and the sugar. Blend until smooth.

8. **Enjoy!** Serve your soup with your tasty baked grilled cheese sammies.

DID YOU KNOW?

Humans have been enjoying the bread-and-cheese combination since the Roman Empire. That was back in 27 BCE to 476 CE!

Herbed Salmon with Asparagus 👐👐👐

Surprise your family with this sophisticated* dinner tonight.

PREP TIME
5 minutes

COOK TIME
20 minutes

MAKES
6
SERVINGS

GLUTEN-FREE
NUT-FREE

KITCHEN TOOLS YOU WILL NEED

Baking sheet

Parchment paper or aluminum foil

Kid-safe knife

Cutting board

Food processor

Measuring cups

Measuring spoons

Pastry brush or spoon

INGREDIENTS YOU WILL NEED

Olive oil cooking spray

2 pounds **asparagus**

6 (6-ounce) fillets **salmon**, skin on

1½ cups **fresh parsley leaves**

1½ cups **fresh dill fronds**

1 cup **fresh basil leaves**

6 **green onions**, chopped

4 **cloves garlic**

Juice of 2 lemons (about 6 tablespoons)

2 tablespoons **honey**

1 tablespoon **olive oil**

¼ teaspoon **salt**

½ teaspoon **freshly ground black pepper**

JUST FOR LAUGHS

What do you call a salmon wearing a suit and tie?

Sofishticated.

DIRECTIONS

1. 🛑 **Preheat the oven and prepare the pan.** Preheat the oven to 450°F. Line the baking sheet with parchment paper or aluminum foil. Spray the foil with the olive oil.

2.  **Trim* the asparagus.** Cut the hard, woody ends off the asparagus (usually the bottom inch).

3. **Place the salmon and asparagus on the baking sheet.** Lay the salmon fillets skin-side down in the middle of the prepared baking sheet. Arrange the asparagus around the salmon.

 **Sophisticated:** Fancy.

Trim: Cutting off the inedible part of the fruit or vegetable. In this recipe, you'll be removing the hard, woody part of the asparagus.

4. Blend the seasoning. (STOP) In the bowl of the food processor, combine the parsley, dill, basil, green onions, garlic, lemon juice, honey, olive oil, salt, and pepper. Blend until smooth.

5. Brush* **the salmon with the herb paste.** Using a pastry brush, paint the salmon thickly with the herb paste. Brush a bit on top of the asparagus as well.

6. Bake. (STOP) Place the pan in the preheated oven. Bake for 10 to 12 minutes, and then carefully remove from the oven. Set the pan aside for 5 minutes to let the salmon finish cooking (you know salmon is done when it is opaque in the middle). Enjoy!

✳ Brush:
Adding a small amount of oil or butter evenly to the surface of the ingredient by using a pastry brush or your fingers.

MAKE IT YOUR OWN

What would make a great side dish with this salmon? Do you want to make extra herb paste for dipping (if you do, be sure to keep it away from the raw fish for safety)? Is there a different vegetable that would be tasty with the salmon?

I MADE IT MY OWN BY:

....

....

....

....

....

Tropical Mocktail *page 90*

Desserts & Drinks

Time for sweets and drinks to sip!
Now, one last tip:
Every day is awesome, each day is new.
As the chef, it's up to you
to create a dish so tasty and fun
to bring smiles to each and every one.
So after cooking, pack it all away
and know tomorrow is another day
full of great tasty food to try.
The possibilities are as high as the sky.

Tropical Mocktail

A lovely beach-side vacation is only a few tablespoons away with this delicious drink.

KITCHEN TOOLS YOU WILL NEED

Tall drinking glass

Measuring spoons

Measuring cup

Mixing spoon

Fancy straw (optional)

INGREDIENTS YOU WILL NEED

Ice cubes

2 tablespoons **fresh lemon juice**

2 tablespoons **100% cranberry juice**

2 tablespoons **pineapple juice**

1 tablespoon **orange juice concentrate**

½ cup **club soda**

PREP TIME
5 minutes

MAKES
1
SERVING

DAIRY-FREE
GLUTEN-FREE
NUT-FREE
VEGAN
VEGETARIAN

DIRECTIONS

1. **Add ice to the glass.** The perfect glass will be see-through so you can see all the colors.

2. **Prepare the drink.** Pour the lemon juice, cranberry juice, pineapple juice, and orange juice concentrate over the ice. Stir with the spoon and add a fancy straw if you have one. Enjoy!

 **DID YOU KNOW?**

Many people believe that cranberries are grown in water, but cranberries are actually grown on vines in sandy bogs or marshes. Because cranberries float, these areas are flooded during harvest time so the ripe berries float to the surface, which makes them easier to harvest. Have you ever seen a cranberry bog?

 I MADE THIS
RECIPE ON:
(DATE)

- - - - - - - - - - - - - - - - - -

 IT TASTED:
(CIRCLE
THE STARS)

 ★ ★ ★ ★ ★

 WHO
HELPED?

- - - - - - - - - - - - - - - - - -

- - - - - - - - - - - - - - - - - -

- - - - - - - - - - - - - - - - - -

- - - - - - - - - - - - - - - - - -

JUST FOR
LAUGHS

What's small, round, and blue?

A cranberry holding its breath.

Frozen Yogurt Bark

What is cold and creamy, sweet and tart, and super refreshing on a hot day? Frozen yogurt bark.

PREP TIME
10 minutes

FREEZE TIME
2 to 4 hours

MAKES
6
SERVINGS

NUT-FREE
VEGETARIAN

KITCHEN TOOLS YOU WILL NEED

Medium mixing bowl

Measuring cup

Measuring spoon

Rimmed baking sheet

Wax paper

Mixing spoon

Sharp knife

INGREDIENTS YOU WILL NEED

2 cups **full-fat Greek yogurt** (or non-dairy alternative)

2 tablespoons **pure maple syrup**

½ teaspoon **pure vanilla extract**

½ cup **toppings** of your choice: sliced strawberries, blueberries, shredded coconut, dark chocolate shavings, cranberries, raisins, crushed nuts, hulled hemp seeds, ½ teaspoon lemon zest

I MADE THIS
RECIPE ON:
(DATE)

- -

IT TASTED:
(CIRCLE
THE STARS)

★ ★ ★ ★ ★

WHO
HELPED?

- -

- -

- -

- -

JUST FOR
LAUGHS

**What's a pilot's
favorite kind
of yogurt?**

Plain.

DIRECTIONS

1. Prepare the bark. In the medium bowl, combine the yogurt, maple syrup, and vanilla.

2. Prepare the baking sheet. Line the rimmed baking sheet with wax paper.

3. Pour the yogurt into the prepared baking sheet. Pour the yogurt mixture into the prepared baking sheet and spread evenly (ideally not thicker than ½ inch in any area).

4. **Add the toppings.** Sprinkle your chosen toppings on top of the yogurt mixture.

5. **Freeze.** Place the pan in the freezer for 2 to 4 hours until the bark has hardened. (STOP) Using a sharp knife, break the bark into pieces. Enjoy!

Watermelon Mint Lemonade on the Half-Rind 👐

Is it party time? It's always party time with this fun drink, served on the half-rind.*

KITCHEN TOOLS YOU WILL NEED

Sharp knife

Plastic wrap

Large spoon

Large mixing bowl

Measuring cups

Immersion blender

Fine-mesh sieve

INGREDIENTS YOU WILL NEED

½ of a 20-pound seedless **watermelon** (not a 10-pound melon)

¾ cup **water**

¾ cup **white sugar**

1½ cups **fresh lemon juice**

¾ cup loosely packed **mint leaves**

PREP TIME
15 minutes

CHILL TIME
20 minutes

MAKES

9

SERVINGS

DAIRY-FREE
GLUTEN-FREE
NUT-FREE
VEGAN
VEGETARIAN

**JUST FOR
LAUGHS**

**When is the only time
you go at red and
stop at green?**

When you eat
a watermelon!

DIRECTIONS

1. 🛑 **Prepare the melon.** Cut the watermelon in half, lengthwise. Then cut a thin slice from the bottom of one half of the melon to allow it to sit flat. (Wrap and refrigerate the other half for another day.)

2. Scoop the fruit. Using the large spoon, scoop 15 cups of watermelon fruit into the large mixing bowl. Save the empty watermelon half to serve your drink. (It will act as your "boat".)

3. Add the remaining ingredients. To the same bowl, add the water, sugar, lemon juice, and mint.

✳ **Half-rind:**
A melon skin is called a "rind." When you cut a melon in half and scoop out the fruit, what's left is the green and white half-rind.

4. **Blend.** Using an immersion blender, blend the watermelon mixture until smooth.

5. Strain.* Pour the liquid through a fine-mesh sieve and into the reserved watermelon boat.

6. **Refrigerate.** Cover the filled watermelon with plastic wrap. Carefully place in the refrigerator and chill for 20 minutes before serving. Enjoy!

MAKE IT YOUR OWN

What flavor do you want to try next? Tropical mango? Tart cherry? Lasagna? (Okay, that last one was a joke.)

I MADE IT MY OWN BY:

? DID YOU KNOW?

There are 1,200 different varieties of watermelon. In China, people enjoy stir-fried or stewed watermelon rinds, but in the American South, cooks pickle the rind. Across the Middle East and China, watermelon seeds are dried and roasted, like pumpkin seeds!

✱ Strain:

Separating liquid from particles or other solids in order to remove pieces that you don't want in the dish.

Summertime Roasted Fruit

This is the ultimate side dish—or dessert. Eat it on top of pancakes, waffles, ice cream, yogurt, or oatmeal.

PREP TIME
5 minutes

COOK TIME
40 minutes

MAKES
8
SERVINGS

DAIRY-FREE
GLUTEN-FREE
NUT-FREE
VEGAN
VEGETARIAN

KITCHEN TOOLS YOU WILL NEED

Baking sheet

Aluminum foil

Measuring spoons

INGREDIENTS YOU WILL NEED

Olive oil cooking spray

16 ounces **frozen peaches**

12 ounces **frozen blueberries**

1 tablespoon **brown sugar**

¼ teaspoon **ground cinnamon**

I MADE THIS
RECIPE ON:
(DATE)

- -

IT TASTED:
(CIRCLE
THE STARS)

WHO
HELPED?

- -

- -

- -

JUST FOR
LAUGHS

Did you hear about the fruit that gave people a warm fuzzy feeling all over?

She was a real peach.

DIRECTIONS

1. 🛑 **Preheat the oven and prepare the pan.** Preheat the oven to 400°F. Line the baking sheet with aluminum foil. Spray the foil lightly with the oil.

2. **Prepare the fruit.** Arrange the peaches and blueberries in a single layer on the prepared baking sheet. Sprinkle with the sugar and cinnamon.

3. Roast. (STOP) Place the pan in the preheated oven and roast the fruit for 30 minutes. Remove the pan from the oven and let cool for 10 minutes before serving. Enjoy!

? DID YOU KNOW?

The world's largest peach is in Gaffney, South Carolina. It weighs over 10,000 pounds . . . but don't try to take a bite! This mega-peach is actually the Gaffney city water tower. The world's heaviest real, edible peach was picked in July 2018 and weighed 1.8 pounds—that's 5½ times bigger than the average peach.

MAKE IT YOUR OWN

This recipe would taste great with plums, pears, or even peeled apple slices. What will you try first?

I MADE IT MY OWN BY:

Raspberry Lemon Mug Cake

The perfect single-serving dessert is minutes away with this delicious mug cake.

PREP TIME
5 minutes

COOK TIME
5 minutes

MAKES
1
SERVING

NUT-FREE
VEGETARIAN

KITCHEN TOOLS YOU WILL NEED

Microwave-safe coffee mug

Measuring spoons

Chopstick or fork

INGREDIENTS YOU WILL NEED

3 tablespoons **all-purpose flour**

2 tablespoons **white sugar**

¼ teaspoon **baking powder**

2 tablespoons **whole milk** or non-dairy alternative

1 teaspoon **softened unsalted butter**

2 teaspoons **full-fat sour cream**

1 tablespoon **fresh lemon juice**

¼ teaspoon **pure vanilla extract**

1 tablespoon **raspberry jam**

 I MADE THIS
RECIPE ON:
(DATE)

 IT TASTED:
(CIRCLE
THE STARS)

★ ★ ★ ★ ★

 WHO
HELPED?

 JUST FOR
LAUGHS

What did the cake say to the fork?

Do you want a piece of me?

DIRECTIONS

1. Mix the dry ingredients. In the mug, combine the flour, sugar, and baking powder. Using the chopstick or a small fork, stir well.

2. Add the wet ingredients. To the mug, add the milk, butter, sour cream, lemon juice, and vanilla. Stir until well combined, being sure to use the chopstick or fork to get to any dry ingredients that may be stuck around the bottom of the mug.

3. Swirl in the raspberry jam. Add a spoonful of the raspberry jam on top of the batter. Using the chopstick or fork, slowly stir 2 to 3 times to swirl it into the batter.

4. Cook. Place the mug in the microwave. Cook on High for 1½ minutes. STOP Carefully remove the mug from the microwave. Let it cool for 4 minutes before serving. Enjoy!

 MAKE IT YOUR OWN

Replace the raspberry jam with fresh berries or with another kind of berry jam. What's your favorite?

I MADE IT MY OWN BY:

COOKING WITH KIDS 101:
A GUIDE FOR GROWN-UPS

Cooking with kids has many benefits: It helps open cautious ("picky") eaters to new foods. It helps children build ownership, self-esteem, and confidence. And it's a great way to teach kids about where food comes from. Here are a few tips to make the wonderful art of cooking fun and safe for your children.

KITCHEN HACKS

When I started cooking with my twins, and then in my class, Toddler Test Kitchen™, I learned that starting out small and growing is the way to go. By starting with simple tasks—such as using little hands to tear lettuce for a salad, or helping stir ingredients in a pot (using a kitchen stool to reach the stove)—kids and their grown-up sous-chefs can grow in confidence together.

Often, parents underrate their children's abilities in the kitchen. From a young age, they can help measure ingredients and use a kid-safe knife to cut vegetables and fruits. By starting early and advancing with your comfort level, you are setting your little chef up for kitchen independence.

Here are some of the most effective cooking hacks for helping a little one become a mini chef.

- Put a rubber band at the level on the measuring cup that you want kids to measure to.

- Have kids crack eggs into a bowl and fish out the shells (rather than crack into the recipe).

- Use bowls, pots, and pans that are bigger than needed, so there's extra room for a child's enthusiastic stirring.

- Practice knife skills with a banana and butter knife or a kid-safe knife. You can use a butter knife to cut lettuce, spinach, zucchini, and other soft vegetables.

- Set up a sturdy, non-slip stool so kids can reach things.

- Always let your child do any assembly required—it may not be perfect, but it's so much more fun!

- If thin slices of a vegetable are needed, your child can use a vegetable peeler instead of a knife.

- Use an apple slicer to easily core and slice an apple.

- Use a vegetable chopper to cut vegetables into small, diced cubes.

- If there are multiple kids, assign tasks ahead of time.

TEACHING SHARPS, STOVETOP, AND OVEN SKILLS

Kitchen safety is an important skill to learn. With the proper tools and rules, you can set your child up for success and safety in the kitchen.

Real Knives vs. Kid-Safe Knives

Real knives are sharp and heavy. Kid-safe knives can cut ingredients just like a "real" knife, but they are smaller, easy to hold, and often have a serrated but blunt tip.

When your child is first starting out, you might want them to try a nylon serrated knife, which has the weight, shape, and feel of a chef's knife without the sharp edge. The blunt, serrated knife makes cutting ingredients possible without any risk of cuts. Or try a wavy crinkle-cut knife, which cuts ingredients without a sharp blade. After your child masters that, move to smaller real knives, like a paring knife. These knives can cut tiny hands, so monitor your child closely when they're using one. If you are very concerned about cuts, purchase no-cut gloves for your child to use when handling knives. Here are some tips for teaching your child knife skills.

- Have your child practice rocking the knife from tip to end when cutting. This will help keep the knife from slipping.

- Teach your child to hold their fingers in a claw shape (keeping fingertips away from the blade) and to move their fingers and watch carefully as they move the knife down to cut an ingredient.

- Explain that food is easier to cut when it has a flat, stable surface. Begin by cutting food in half or slicing off a part to create a flat side of the food to set your child up for safe cutting.

- Make sure your child is at the right height to get sufficient leverage over the food they are cutting. Use a non-slip stool if necessary.

- Build confidence by starting out with soft foods that are easy to cut and using a kid-safe knife or butter knife.

Graters and Peelers

A box grater or a vegetable peeler can be just as sharp as a knife. It's important to take things slow. Here are some tips for teaching skills with graters and peelers.

- Teach your child to grate and peel only in one direction (down or away from the body). Start with a long vegetable. Teach your child to hold one end in their non-dominant hand, and with the other hand, peel away from their body.

- Teach your child to grate using big pieces and to stop before they get to the end of the ingredient. When grating cheese, keep it extra cold and have them grip the top, leaving plenty of room between their fingers and the grater.

- Describe grating or peeling like petting a cat or dog—with soft, gentle strokes.

Using the Stovetop

You may not feel comfortable letting your child use the stovetop by themselves, and that's okay! Even if your child isn't using the stove on their own, it's helpful for children to understand basic stove safety. Here are some tips to teach your child about using the stovetop.

- Tell them you use back burners first, so hot pots are further from the edge. Explain that you always turn pot handles so they're not hanging over the edge. This will prevent someone from knocking into the pot and spilling it.

- Explain that you never leave a stovetop unattended when it's on, and don't leave empty pans on hot burners.

- Discuss the importance of checking for body safety: Tie back long hair, roll up long sleeves, keep loose clothing away from the stove, and be sure the kitchen stool and footwear are non-slip.

- Talk about the importance of being very careful with hot oil. Step back so it doesn't splatter on you.

Using the Oven

The same rules that apply to using the stovetop also apply to the oven. Here are some tips to discuss when introducing oven skills.

- Emphasize that they should never touch oven racks with their bare hands. Let your child know that you keep heat-proof potholders and oven mitts around.

- Teach your child not to touch oven doors, as they can get hot.

- Explain that it's important to stand far back when you open the oven door, especially when something may be steaming inside.

- Discuss the proper order for checking cooking progress: First, put oven mitts on; then open the door; and then pull out the oven rack.

- Teach children to move slowly and to avoid sudden movements to avoid bumps or falls near an open oven.

MEASUREMENT CONVERSIONS

Volume Equivalents (LIQUID)

US STANDARD	US STANDARD (OUNCES)	METRIC (APPROXIMATE)
2 tablespoons	1 fl. oz.	30 mL
¼ cup	2 fl. oz.	60 mL
½ cup	4 fl. oz.	120 mL
1 cup	8 fl. oz.	240 mL
1½ cups	12 fl. oz.	355 mL
2 cups or 1 pint	16 fl. oz.	475 mL
4 cups or 1 quart	32 fl. oz.	1 L
1 gallon	128 fl. oz.	4 L

Oven Temperatures

FAHRENHEIT (F)	CELSIUS (C) (APPROXIMATE)
250°F	120°C
300°F	150°C
325°F	165°C
350°F	180°C
375°F	190°C
400°F	200°C
425°F	220°C
450°F	230°C

Volume Equivalents (DRY)

US STANDARD	METRIC (APPROXIMATE)
⅛ teaspoon	0.5 mL
¼ teaspoon	1 mL
½ teaspoon	2 mL
¾ teaspoon	4 mL
1 teaspoon	5 mL
1 tablespoon	15 mL
¼ cup	59 mL
⅓ cup	79 mL
½ cup	118 mL
⅔ cup	156 mL
¾ cup	177 mL
1 cup	235 mL
2 cups or 1 pint	475 mL
3 cups	700 mL
4 cups or 1 quart	1 L

Weight Equivalents

US STANDARD	METRIC (APPROXIMATE)
½ ounce	15 g
1 ounce	30 g
2 ounces	60 g
4 ounces	115 g
8 ounces	225 g
12 ounces	340 g
16 ounces or 1 pound	455 g

INDEX

ACKNOWLEDGMENTS

First and foremost, the Lev of my life. It may sound fishy, but you're my sole mate.

Shimon, Benjamin, and Daniel. You have been my joy, my pride, and my sunshine. Neil Diamond said, "Good times never seem so good," but I disagree. These are good times. And I know it.

My parents, Joan and Lenny Kalmenson, the best grandparents.

Brian Kalmenson and Casey Sorrell, for sharing in my accomplishments and inundating your friends with my collection of works. I am grateful. I hope your friends are, too.

Shoshi. My co-mom. Everyone needs that friend who holds your hand and makes you feel like you can take on the world. I'm a better mother, wife, and friend because of the time we have spent together.

And as always, to the best editor, Laura Apperson. We were thrown together over a love of words and food, and we've certainly run with it. Thank you for everything.

ABOUT THE AUTHOR

Yaffi Lvova, RDN, is a registered dietitian nutritionist and owner of Baby Bloom Nutrition® and Toddler Test Kitchen™.

Yaffi is a mother to twins plus one. She has used her experience and clinical knowledge to provide nutrition education to new and expecting parents, and to help smooth the transition into parenthood.

You can find Yaffi at **BabyBloomNutrition.com**; on Facebook, **@BabyBloomNutrition** and **@Toddler TestKitchenAZ**; and on Instagram, **@toddler.testkitchen**.

Other Books by Yaffi Lvova

Discover Mindful Eating for Kids, 2nd edition
Stage-by-Stage Baby Food Cookbook
Beyond a Bite
Nourishing Baby Food Cookbook
Fun with Food Toddler Cookbook
Beyond a Bite Professional Edition (Neurodiverse edition)
Beyond a Bite Parent Edition (Neurodiverse edition)

discover more in the
kid chef
series

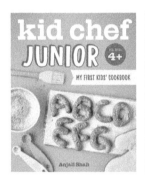

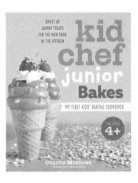

Kid Chef Junior
My First Kids' Cookbook

Anjali Shah

978-1-64152-135-2

$14.99 US / $19.99 CAN

Kid Chef
The Foodie Kids' Cookbook:
Healthy Recipes and Culinary
Skills for the New Cook
in the Kitchen

Melina Hammer

978-1-94345-120-3

$15.99 US / $19.99 CAN

Kid Chef Junior Bakes
My First Kids
Baking Cookbook:
Sweet & Savory Treats for the
New Cook in the Kitchen

Charity Mathews

978-1-64152-529-9

$14.99 US / $19.99 CAN

Kid Chef Every Day
The Easy Cookbook
for Foodie Kids: Simple
Recipes and Essential
Techniques to Wow
Your Family

Colleen Kennedy

978-1-64152-222-9

$16.99 US / $22.99 CAN

ROCKRIDGE PRESS

Available wherever books and ebooks are sold

Printed in the USA
CPSIA information can be obtained
at www.ICGtesting.com
CBHW040753100424
6610CB00001B/3